Fathering Strong Fatherhood Workshop Facilitator Guide

BRUCE STAPLETON

Table of Contents

Foreword from the Author

Dear Workshop Facilitator,

Thank you for taking up the torch of leading men toward stronger, more intentional fatherhood. The guide you hold in your hands represents not just a curriculum but a vision for transforming families and communities through the influence of faithful fathers.

My journey to creating the Fathering Strong Fatherhood Workshop began at the crossroads of my professional and personal life. As a business leader, I witnessed how strategic planning and intentional leadership transformed organizations. As an educator, I saw how a well-designed curriculum could facilitate genuine change in students' thinking and behavior. As a father, I experienced firsthand the profound joys and sobering challenges of raising children in today's complex world.

But it was in my struggles as a father that the seeds of Fathering Strong were planted. Despite my leadership experience, I often felt unprepared for the most important leadership role of all—guiding my family. I found myself reacting to situations rather than proactively leading, unsure of how to translate my professional skills into effective fatherhood. Through prayer, Scripture study, and intentional practice, I began to see how the principles of courageous leadership could be applied at home. The transformation in my family relationships was profound, and I became convinced that other fathers needed a structured pathway to similar growth.

This Facilitator's Guide represents years of refining those insights into a practical, reproducible format. It's designed not just to convey information but to facilitate transformation. As you lead men through these twelve weeks, you're providing them with both the biblical foundation and practical tools to become the fathers God designed them to be.

Your Role As Facilitator

Your role as facilitator is crucial. While the curriculum provides structure, it's your authentic leadership and engagement that will bring it to life. Don't feel pressured to have all the answers or to present yourself as the perfect father. Instead, approach each session as a fellow traveler on the fatherhood journey, willing to share both your successes and your struggles. Your vulnerability will create space for genuine sharing among participants.

Remember that the men in your group are at different stages in their faith journey and fatherhood experience. Some may have deep wounds from their own fathers that need healing before they can fully embrace their role. Others may be hungry for practical tools to implement immediately. The structured flexibility of this curriculum allows you to honor these differences while guiding everyone toward growth.

As you begin this journey, I encourage you to start with prayer for each participant by name. Ask God to prepare their hearts, to bring healing where needed, and to give you discernment in leading discussions. Trust that even when sessions don't go exactly as planned, God is at work beneath the surface, shaping these men into the fathers He has called them to be.

The impact of your leadership will extend far beyond the men in your group. As these fathers implement what they learn, their children will experience greater security and spiritual nurture. Their marriages will likely strengthen. Their churches and communities will benefit from their more intentional presence. Generations yet unborn may be influenced by the legacy these men establish. What a privilege to be part of such a far-reaching ministry!

Thank you for your willingness to serve in this capacity. May God bless your efforts abundantly as you equip His sons to raise the next generation of faithful men and women.

My Prayer for You as the Facilitator

As you begin your journey as the facilitator, know that we are praying for you and the fathers in your group. The work you're about to undertake is holy ground—you'll witness breakthroughs, moments of vulnerability, and the quiet transformation of men becoming the fathers God designed them to be. In those moments when you feel inadequate or uncertain, remember that the Lord doesn't call the equipped; He equips the called. This prayer reflects our heart for your ministry and the sacred trust you've accepted in guiding these fathers.

Heavenly Father,

We come before You with humble hearts, recognizing that the task of guiding fathers is both a privilege and a sacred responsibility. As facilitators of the Fathering Strong Fatherhood Workshop, we ask for Your divine wisdom and discernment.

Lord, equip us with patience, understanding, and the ability to listen deeply to the men You've entrusted to our care. When discussions become challenging, or emotions run high, grant us the right words and a spirit of grace.

Father, we ask that You work through our inadequacies and strengthen our weaknesses. Help us to model authentic fatherhood even as we guide others. Where we have our own unresolved wounds or blind spots, bring gentle healing and revelation.

Give us discernment to recognize the unique needs of each participant. Show us when to speak and when to remain silent, when to challenge, and when to comfort.

May our leadership reflect Your perfect fatherhood, and may every session be filled with Your presence and power. Let transformation begin in our own hearts first so that we might lead not just from knowledge but from lived experience.

We surrender this workshop and these fathers to You, trusting that You will accomplish Your purposes in their lives and families.

In the name of Jesus, our ultimate example, Amen.

May your faithful service as a facilitator ignite a movement of godly fatherhood that transforms families for generations to come.

For stronger families and future generations,

Bruce Stapleton
Author, Fathering Strong: God's Blueprint for Leading Your Family

Introduction

Welcome to the Fathering Strong Workshop Facilitator's Guide. This comprehensive resource is designed to equip you with everything needed to lead fathers through a transformative 12-week journey of growth and development. As a facilitator, you play a crucial role in creating an environment where men can explore their calling as fathers, develop practical skills, and build a supportive community beyond the workshop.

This guide provides detailed session outlines, teaching points, discussion prompts, and practical tips for facilitating meaningful conversations and activities. Each week builds upon previous sessions, creating a cohesive path toward stronger, more intentional fatherhood for your participants.

Remember that your role is not to have all the answers but to guide the process of discovery and growth. Your authentic leadership, vulnerability, and commitment to your own fatherhood journey will set the tone for the group. Trust the process, rely on the materials provided, and, most importantly, depend on God's guidance as you lead these fathers toward a stronger vision of fatherhood.

Preparation for Facilitators

Before the Workshop Begins:

➤ Take time to thoroughly review all materials, including the Participant Workbook, the book *Fathering Strong – God's Blueprint for Leading Your Family*, and the *30-Day Devotional and Journal*. Familiarize yourself with the overall flow and objectives of each session.

➤ Pray specifically for each registered participant by name. Ask God to prepare their hearts for transformation and to give you wisdom in leading them.

➤ Set up a communication system for the group (email list, messaging app, etc.) to share reminders and encouragement between sessions.

➤ Prepare the meeting space to be welcoming and conducive to both teaching and small group discussion. Consider the seating arrangement, lighting, and any technology needs.

➤ Gather necessary supplies: name tags, extra pens, blank paper, and any visual aids you plan to use.

➤ Consider recruiting a co-facilitator or small group leader if your group exceeds 12 participants. This ensures everyone receives personal attention and has ample opportunity to share.

For Each Session:

➤ Review the specific session content at least two days before meeting. Make a note of key teaching points, scripture references, and discussion questions.

➤ Pray for discernment about which personal examples or stories might enhance the teaching points. Authentic vulnerability from you sets the tone for the group.

➤ Prepare any handouts, visual aids, or technology needed for the specific session.

➤ Arrive early to set up the room and greet participants as they arrive. Creating a welcoming atmosphere begins before the formal session starts.

Session Time Management

Standard 60-Minute Format

Each session in this guide is designed for a 60-minute timeframe, making it ideal for Sunday morning men's groups or other weekly gatherings where time may be limited. The standard time breakdown is as follows:

➢ **Welcome & Check-in (5 minutes)**: Brief greeting and connection point
➢ **Core Teaching & Discussion (40 minutes)**: Presentation of key concepts and guided discussion
➢ **Application Exercise (10 minutes)**: Practical activity to reinforce learning
➢ **Next Steps & Closing (5 minutes)**: Assignment overview and closing prayer

Extending Your Sessions

While the 60-minute format provides a complete experience, many groups benefit from extended engagement with the material. Each session contains 2-3 Key Teaching Points that can serve as natural breaking points for expanding into multiple meetings:

➢ **Option 1: Extended Single Session (90 minutes)**
  o Increase discussion time for each Key Teaching Point
  o Allow 20-25 minutes for the Application Exercise
  o Include refreshment/fellowship time
➢ **Option 2: Split Session Format (Two 45-60 minute meetings)**
  o First Meeting: Cover Welcome, Key Teaching Point 1, and begin Key Teaching Point 2
  o Second Meeting: Review, complete Key Teaching Point 2, Key Teaching Point 3, and Application Exercise

Adapting to Your Group's Needs

Pay attention to which topics resonate most deeply with your specific group of fathers. You may choose to:

➢ Spend additional time on particularly relevant Key Teaching Points
➢ Incorporate supplemental discussion questions from the Participant Workbook
➢ Add testimony time where fathers can share their experiences with implementing the previous week's principles

Remember that transformation happens not just through information but through reflection and application. Creating space for both is essential to the Fathering Strong experience.

General Facilitation Tips

Creating a Safe Environment:

➤ Establish clear ground rules in the first session: confidentiality, respect for different perspectives, no interrupting, and the value of active listening.

➤ Model vulnerability by appropriately sharing your own fatherhood journey, including both successes and challenges.

➤ Affirm participants' contributions, even when they differ from your perspective or experience.

➤ Address any disrespectful comments or dominating behaviors privately and promptly.

Facilitating Meaningful Discussions:

➤ Use open-ended questions that require more than yes/no answers.

➤ Become comfortable with silence. Allow 5-10 seconds after asking a question before rephrasing or moving on.

➤ Draw out quieter participants with direct but gentle invitations: "John, I'd be interested in your thoughts on this."

➤ Manage more talkative participants by acknowledging their contribution and then redirecting: "Thanks for that insight, Mike. I'd like to hear from someone who hasn't shared yet."

➤ Connect participants' comments to the larger themes of the session: "What you're describing relates directly to the courage we discussed earlier."

Managing Time Effectively:

➤ Start and end on time, respecting participants' schedules.

➤ Be prepared to adjust on the fly. If a particular discussion is especially meaningful, allow it to continue and abbreviate a less critical section.

➤ Use gentle transitions between segments: "We have about five minutes left for this discussion before moving to our small group activity."

➤ Keep a visible clock or set quiet timer alerts on your phone to help track time without constantly checking your watch.

Handling Challenging Situations:

➤ For the participant who dominates: "Thanks for sharing, Bob. Let's hear from someone who hasn't had a chance to speak yet."

➤ For the participant who challenges everything: "That's an interesting perspective. Let's hold that thought and discuss it further during the break."

➤ For emotional moments: "Thank you for being vulnerable. This is exactly the kind of authentic sharing that helps us all grow."

➤ For off-topic tangents: "That's an important point that might be better addressed in our session on [relevant topic]. Let's make a note to revisit it then."

Workshop Materials Checklist

For the Facilitator:

➢ Facilitator's Guide (this document)

➢ Participant Workbook (for reference)

➢ Fathering Strong – God's Blueprint for Leading Your Family book

➢ Fathering Strong – 30-Day Devotional and Journal

➢ Whiteboard or flip chart and markers

➢ Laptop/projector if using visual presentations

➢ Timer or watch

➢ Name tags for the first few sessions

For Each Participant:

➢ Participant Workbook

➢ ***Fathering Strong – God's Blueprint for Leading Your Family*** book

➢ Fathering Strong – 30-Day Devotional and Journal *(optional – can also download 7-Day Fatherhood Awakening exercises on the website www.fatheringstrongbook.com)*

➢ Pen

➢ Name tag (first session)

Week 1: The Call to Fathering Strong

Session Preparation

Room Setup: Arrange seating in a circle or U-shape to facilitate conversation. If using small groups, ensure there are designated areas where groups can talk without excessive noise overlap.

Materials Needed:

> - Name tags
> - Participant Workbooks
> - Pens
> - Whiteboard or flip chart
> - Markers
> - Optional: Light refreshments

Pre-Session Checklist:

> - Review teaching content and discussion questions
> - Prepare personal examples that illustrate key points
> - Set up room and any technology
> - Arrange refreshments if provided

Session Outline (60 minutes)

Welcome & Introduction (10 minutes instead of standard 5)

> - Welcome participants and introduce yourself, sharing briefly about your fatherhood journey and why you're facilitating this workshop.
> - Have participants introduce themselves: name, number, and ages of children, and one hope they have for this workshop.
> - Explain the workshop format and expectations: weekly meetings, reading assignments, practical application, and the importance of confidentiality.
> - Distribute Participant Workbooks and explain how they'll be used throughout the 12 weeks.

Core Teaching & Discussion (30 minutes)

Key Teaching Point 1: Fatherhood as a Divine Calling (7-8 minutes)
Explain the difference between viewing fatherhood as merely a role versus a sacred calling from God.

Scripture focus: Ephesians 3:14-15 – "For this reason I kneel before the Father, from whom every family in heaven and on earth derives its name."

Discussion prompt: "How does viewing fatherhood as a divine calling rather than just a responsibility change your perspective?"

Key Teaching Point 2: The Four Pillars of Fathering Strong (7-8 minutes)
Introduce and briefly explain each pillar:

- ➤ **Courage:** The strength to face challenges and make difficult decisions
- ➤ **Fortitude:** The persistence to stay the course through difficulties
- ➤ **Faith:** The trust in God's guidance and promises
- ➤ **Love:** The sacrificial commitment to your family's wellbeing

Scripture focus: 1 Corinthians 16:13-14 – "Be on your guard; stand firm in the faith; be courageous; be strong. Do everything in love."

Discussion prompt: "Which of these four pillars feels like a strength for you, and which might need development?"

Key Teaching Point 3: Success vs. Significance (7-8 minutes) Contrast culture's definition of successful fatherhood (providing material, achievements, etc.) with significance-focused fatherhood (character development, spiritual leadership, relational connection).

Personal example: Share a brief story illustrating how you've navigated this tension in your own fatherhood journey.

Discussion prompt: "What messages about 'successful fatherhood' have influenced you, and how do they compare with God's perspective?"

Small Group Application Exercise (10 minutes)

- • Divide into groups of 3-4 fathers.
- • Have each person share: "Where are you currently in your fatherhood journey? What brought you to this workshop?"
- • Encourage them to note similarities and differences in their experiences.

Next Steps & Assignment Overview (10 minutes instead of standard 5)

- ➤ Review the reading assignment for next week:
  - ○ Fathering Strong – God's Blueprint for Leading Your Family: Introduction and Chapters 1-2
  - ○ Fathering Strong – 30-Day Devotional and Journal: Introduction and Day 1 of the 7-Day Awakening

- ➤ Explain the importance of completing the reading and reflection questions before the next session.

- ➤ Introduce the fatherhood vision statement they'll begin working on this week.
- ➤ Answer any questions about the workshop format or expectations.
- ➤ Close with a brief prayer for the journey ahead.

Closing Prayer

Heavenly Father,

We come before You with grateful hearts for bringing each man here today. Thank You for the courage it took for these fathers to commit to this journey of growth.

Lord, we acknowledge that true fatherhood finds its source in You. As we begin this workshop, help us to shift our focus from worldly success to eternal significance in the lives of our children and families.

Give us wisdom to discern Your blueprint for fatherhood. Open our hearts to Your teaching, our minds to new perspectives, and our spirits to transformation.

Strengthen the bonds forming in this room today. May the community we build here become a source of encouragement, accountability, and support.

Guide us in the week ahead as we begin our readings and reflections. Help us to carve out the time needed to engage deeply with these materials.

We surrender our fatherhood journeys to You, asking that You would make us the fathers You've designed us to be.

In Jesus' name, we pray, Amen.

Facilitation Notes and Tips

For the Welcome & Introduction: The first session sets the tone for the entire workshop. Be especially warm and welcoming, acknowledging the courage it takes to commit to a fatherhood growth journey.

If the group seems hesitant or quiet, share a brief, appropriate, humorous story about your own fatherhood journey to break the ice.

For the Core Teaching: Watch participants' body language to gauge engagement and understanding. Adjust your pace or examples if needed.

When asking discussion questions, be prepared with follow-up prompts if conversation lags: "Can anyone share a specific example?" or "How might this look in everyday family life?"

For the Small Group Exercise: If some groups finish early, provide an additional prompt: "What's one specific area of fatherhood where you hope to grow through this workshop?"

Circulate among groups, listening briefly to each to ensure they're on track, but don't hover or interrupt their sharing.

For the Next Steps: Emphasize that the reading assignments are crucial for getting the most from the workshop. However, reassure participants that if they can't complete everything, they should still attend—partial preparation is better than missing a session.

Potential Challenges and Solutions

Challenge: Participants are hesitant to share in the first session.
Solution: Start with lower-risk sharing opportunities. Instead of open-ended questions to the whole group, use pair shares or structured responses like, "Share one word that describes your hope for this workshop."

Challenge: Wide range of fatherhood experiences in the room (new dads to grandfathers).
Solution: Acknowledge the diversity as a strength. Note that each perspective brings valuable insights, and all can learn from each other regardless of experience level.

Challenge: Participant expresses skepticism about the spiritual aspects of the workshop.
Solution: Acknowledge their perspective respectfully. Explain that while the workshop has a biblical foundation, the practical principles benefit fathers regardless of their spiritual journey, and they're welcome to engage at their comfort level.

Week 2: God as Father – Our Perfect Model

Session Preparation

Room Setup: Same as Week 1, seating arranged to facilitate conversation.

Materials Needed:

➢ Participant Workbooks

➢ Whiteboard or flip chart

➢ Markers

➢ Optional: Visual aid showing the four roles of God as Father (Protector, Order Keeper, Provider, Stabilizer)

Pre-Session Checklist:

➢ Review participant names if needed

➢ Pray for the session and participants

➢ Review teaching content and discussion questions

➢ Prepare personal examples that illustrate key points

➢ Set up room and any technology

Session Outline (60 minutes)

Welcome & Check-in (5 minutes)

➢ Warmly welcome everyone back.

➢ Brief check-in: "In one sentence, share something you noticed about your fathering this past week after our first session."

➢ Remind the group of confidentiality and the importance of creating a safe space for sharing.

Review of Previous Week's Assignment (10 minutes)

➢ Ask: "What insights stood out to you from the reading assignment?"

➢ Invite 2-3 participants to share initial thoughts on their fatherhood vision statement.

➢ Address any questions that arose from the reading.

Core Teaching & Discussion (30 minutes)

Key Teaching Point 1: God's Four Essential Roles as Father (10 minutes)

Explain each role with biblical examples:

➢ Protector: God shields us from harm and fights for us (Psalm 91:1-2)

➢ Order Keeper: God establishes boundaries for our good (Proverbs 3:1-2)

➢ Provider: God meets our needs abundantly (Philippians 4:19)

➢ Stabilizer: God remains constant amid life's changes (Hebrews 13:8)

Discussion prompt: "Which of these four aspects of God's fatherhood resonates most with you right now, and why?"

Key Teaching Point 2: How God's Fatherhood Reshapes Our Understanding (10 minutes)

• Contrast worldly models of fatherhood with God's perfect example.

- Explain how our experience with our earthly fathers can affect our understanding of God and our own fathering.

Scripture focus: "As a father has compassion on his children, so the LORD has compassion on those who fear him." (Psalm 103:13)

Discussion prompt: "How might your view of God as Father influence your approach to fathering your own children?"

Key Teaching Point 3: Practical Application of God's Character (10 minutes)

Provide concrete examples of how fathers can reflect each aspect of God's character:

➢ Protector: Creating physical and emotional safety
➢ Order Keeper: Establishing consistent, loving boundaries
➢ Provider: Meeting needs beyond just material provision
➢ Stabilizer: Being emotionally consistent and dependable

Personal example: Share a brief story of how understanding God's fatherhood changed your approach in a specific situation.

Discussion prompt: "What is one practical way you could better reflect God's character as Father this week?"

Small Group Application Exercise (10 minutes)

➢ Divide into groups of 3-4.
➢ Have each person share: "Which aspect of God's fatherhood do you find most challenging to emulate, and why?"
➢ Encourage group members to offer supportive insights or suggestions to each other.

Next Steps & Assignment Overview (5 minutes)

➢ Review the reading assignment for next week:
  ○ Fathering Strong – God's Blueprint for Leading Your Family: Chapters 3-4
➢ Remind them to continue developing their fatherhood vision based on biblical principles.
➢ Encourage them to identify one specific area where they can better reflect God's fatherhood in their family this week.
➢ Close with a brief prayer focusing on God's perfect fatherhood as our model.

Closing Prayer

Heavenly Father,

We thank You for revealing Yourself as the perfect Father—our Protector, Provider, Order Keeper, and Stabilizer. Your character gives us the blueprint for our own fatherhood journey.

Lord, where we fall short in reflecting Your character, grant us humility to recognize our weaknesses and strength to grow. Help us to see our children through Your eyes of perfect love and patience.

This week, as each man here attempts to better embody an aspect of Your fatherhood, walk alongside us. When we struggle with consistency, remind us of Your unchanging nature. When we fail to protect, recall to our minds Your perfect shelter. When our provision seems inadequate, show us how You provide in ways beyond the material.

Bind us together as brothers committed to a higher standard of fatherhood—one modeled after You. May our families see glimpses of Your character in our imperfect efforts.

In Jesus' name, Amen.

Facilitation Notes and Tips

For the Welcome & Check-in: If someone shares a challenge they faced during the week, acknowledge it with empathy but keep the check-in moving. You can follow up individually after the session if needed.

For the Review of Previous Week's Assignment: If no one volunteers to share insights from the reading, be prepared with 1-2 key points you can highlight to spark discussion.

For the Core Teaching: Be sensitive when discussing God as Father, as some participants may have had difficult relationships with their earthly fathers. Acknowledge this reality while focusing on how God's perfect fatherhood can heal and redirect our understanding.

Use concrete examples that fathers can relate to in their daily lives. Abstract theological concepts should be grounded in practical application.

For the Small Group Exercise: If groups struggle with the challenge of emulating God's fatherhood, suggest they consider: "When is it hardest for you to be consistent, protective, providing, or stabilizing for your children?"

For the Next Steps: Emphasize that identifying one specific area for improvement is more effective than trying to change everything at once. Encourage realistic, manageable goals.

Potential Challenges and Solutions

Challenge: Participant expresses anger or hurt related to their own father.
Solution: Acknowledge their experience with empathy: "Thank you for sharing that. Many of us have complicated relationships with our fathers." Redirect to how God's perfect fatherhood can provide healing and a new model without dismissing their valid feelings.

Challenge: Theological disagreements arise about God's nature.
Solution: Gently refocus on the practical applications rather than theological debates: "Those are interesting perspectives to consider. For our purposes today, let's focus on how these aspects of God's character can help us become better fathers."

Challenge: Participant feels overwhelmed by the gap between God's perfect fatherhood and their own abilities.
Solution: Emphasize progress over perfection: "None of us will father perfectly like God does. The goal is growth and increasing reflection of His character, not perfection."

Week 3: Courage and Fortitude – Facing Fatherhood Head On

Session Preparation

Room Setup: Same as previous weeks, seating arranged to facilitate conversation.

Materials Needed:
- Participant Workbooks
- Whiteboard or flip chart
- Markers
- Optional: Images representing courage in everyday situations

Pre-Session Checklist:

- Pray for the session and participants
- Review teaching content and discussion questions
- Prepare personal examples that illustrate key points
- Set up room and any technology

Session Outline (60 minutes)

Welcome & Check-in (5 minutes)

- Warmly welcome everyone back.
- Brief check-in: "Share one way you attempted to reflect God's fatherhood in your family this past week."
- Remind the group of the safe space you're creating together.

Review of Previous Week's Assignment (10 minutes)

- Ask: "What insights about God as Father stood out to you from the reading?"
- Invite 2-3 participants to share how they're developing their fatherhood vision based on biblical principles.
- Address any questions that arose from the reading.

Core Teaching & Discussion (30 minutes)

Key Teaching Point 1: Understanding Courage in Fatherhood (10 minutes) Define courage as "doing what needs to be done despite fear" rather than the absence of fear.

Explain how courage enables fathers to:

- Make difficult decisions that may be unpopular
- Have tough conversations with their children
- Stand firm on values when facing cultural pressure
- Admit mistakes and ask for forgiveness

Scripture focus: "Have I not commanded you? Be strong and courageous. Do not be afraid; do not be discouraged, for the LORD your God will be with you wherever you go." (Joshua 1:9)

Discussion prompt: "What situation in your fatherhood journey currently requires the most courage?"

Key Teaching Point 2: Everyday Examples of Fatherhood Courage (10 minutes)
Provide concrete examples of courage in daily fathering:

- Setting boundaries when children push back
- Having age-appropriate conversations about difficult topics
- Making unpopular decisions for your child's wellbeing
- Being vulnerable and authentic with your children

Personal example: Share a brief story of when you needed courage as a father and how you navigated it.

Discussion prompt: "What's one area where you need to exercise more courage in your fatherhood right now?"

Key Teaching Point 3: Developing Fortitude for the Long Journey (10 minutes)
Define fortitude as "the strength of mind that enables a person to encounter danger or bear pain or adversity with courage" – the persistence to stay the course.

Explain how fatherhood is a marathon, not a sprint, requiring:

- Consistency through changing seasons
- Persistence when results aren't immediately visible
- Resilience after failures or setbacks
- Endurance through challenging phases of child development

Scripture focus: "Let us not become weary in doing good, for at the proper time we will reap a harvest if we do not give up." (Galatians 6:9)

Discussion prompt: "What aspect of fatherhood has tested your fortitude the most, and how have you responded?"

Small Group Application Exercise (10 minutes)

- Divide into groups of 3-4.
- Have each person identify one specific situation in their fatherhood that currently requires courage.
- Group members offer support and practical suggestions for approaching that situation.

Next Steps & Assignment Overview (5 minutes)

- Review the reading assignment for next week:
    - Fathering Strong – God's Blueprint for Leading Your Family: Chapters 5-6
    - Fathering Strong – 30-Day Devotional and Journal: Complete Day 2 of the 7-Day Awakening – Fatherhood Assessment

- Explain the importance of the Fatherhood Assessment in identifying areas for growth.

- Encourage them to identify one situation requiring courage that they're currently facing and develop an action plan.

- Close with a prayer for courage and fortitude in their fatherhood journey.

Closing Prayer

Heavenly Father,

We come before You with grateful hearts for the gift of fatherhood. Thank You for modeling what true courage looks like through Your unwavering love and commitment to us.

Lord, we acknowledge that being a father often requires courage we don't feel we possess. Grant us the boldness to lead our families with conviction, even when the path isn't clear. When we face situations that intimidate us—difficult conversations, necessary discipline, or modeling vulnerability—remind us that Your strength is made perfect in our weakness.

Father, we ask for fortitude to persevere through the changing seasons of our children's lives. When we don't see immediate results from our efforts, help us remain consistent. When we stumble or fail, give us the resilience to rise again. During exhausting phases of parenting, sustain us with Your endurance.

As we leave today, plant the truth of Galatians 6:9 deep within our hearts. Let us not grow weary in doing good, knowing that at the proper time, we will reap a harvest if we do not give up.

Bind us together as brothers committed to courageous fatherhood, supporting one another through both victories and challenges.

In Jesus' name, Amen.

Facilitation Notes and Tips

For the Welcome & Check-in: If someone indicates they struggled to apply last week's lesson, affirm their honesty rather than showing disappointment. Growth is a process with ups and downs.

For the Review of Previous Week's Assignment: Listen for misconceptions about God's fatherhood that might need gentle correction or clarification.

For the Core Teaching: When discussing courage, emphasize that it looks different for different fathers based on their personality, family situation, and children's needs. There's no one-size-fits-all approach.

For the fortitude section, acknowledge the reality that fatherhood can be exhausting and discouraging at times. This validates fathers' experiences while encouraging perseverance.

For the Small Group Exercise: If participants struggle to identify situations requiring courage, suggest common scenarios: disciplining a strong-willed child, addressing character issues, having difficult conversations about cultural influences, etc.

For the Next Steps: Remind participants that the Fatherhood Assessment is a tool for growth, not condemnation. It's about identifying areas for development not feeling guilty about shortcomings.

Potential Challenges and Solutions

Challenge: Participant shares a situation requiring courage that seems inappropriate or potentially harmful.

Solution: Without embarrassing them, redirect: "That's a complex situation that might benefit from additional perspective. Could we talk more about that after the session?" Then, provide more appropriate guidance privately.

Challenge: The discussion reveals that a participant is facing a serious family crisis requiring professional help.

Solution: Acknowledge the seriousness of their situation with empathy. After the session, privately provide information about professional resources while maintaining your role as a facilitator, not a counselor.

Challenge: Participants focus exclusively on external challenges rather than internal courage.

Solution: Gently redirect: "Those external challenges are real. How might developing internal courage help you face them differently?"

Week 4: Faith and Love – The Anchoring Core Virtues of a Fathering Strong Life

Session Preparation

Room Setup: Same as previous weeks, with seating arranged to facilitate conversation.

Materials Needed:

➢ Participant Workbooks

➢ Whiteboard or flip chart

➢ Markers

➢ Optional: Visual aid showing the relationship between faith, love, and fatherhood

Pre-Session Checklist:

➢ Pray for the session and participants

➢ Review teaching content and discussion questions

➢ Prepare personal examples that illustrate key points

➢ Set up room and any technology

➢ Session Outline (60 minutes)

Welcome & Check-in (5 minutes)

➢ Warmly welcome everyone back.

➢ Brief check-in: "Share one moment from this past week when you needed courage or fortitude as a father."

➢ Acknowledge that we're now one-third of the way through the workshop journey.

Review of Previous Week's Assignment (10 minutes)

➢ Ask: "What insights about courage and fortitude stood out to you from the reading?"

➢ Invite 2-3 participants to share about the situation they identified that requires courage and their action plan.

➢ Address any questions that arose from the reading or the Fatherhood Assessment.

Core Teaching & Discussion (30 minutes)

Key Teaching Point 1: Faith as the Foundation of Fatherhood (10 minutes)
Define faith in the context of fatherhood:

➢ Trust in God's guidance and promises

➢ Confidence in God's design for family

➢ Belief that your efforts as a father matter eternally

➢ Reliance on God's strength rather than your own

➢ Explain how faith provides:

➢ Direction when the path isn't clear

➢ Strength during challenging seasons

➢ Peace amid uncertainty

➢ Hope when the results aren't immediately visible

Scripture focus: "Now faith is confidence in what we hope for and assurance about what we do not see." (Hebrews 11:1)

Discussion prompt: "How does your faith influence your approach to fatherhood? In what ways does it provide guidance and strength?"

Key Teaching Point 2: Love as Action, Not Just Emotion (10 minutes)
Contrast cultural definitions of love (feelings-based, conditional) with biblical love (action-based, sacrificial, unconditional).

Explain the different expressions of love needed in fatherhood:

- **Affectionate love**: expressing warmth and delight in your children
- **Providing love**: meeting physical, emotional, and spiritual needs
- **Protecting love**: creating boundaries and ensuring safety
- **Instructing love:** guiding and teaching, even when unpopular

Scripture focus: "Love is patient, love is kind... it always protects, always trusts, always hopes, always perseveres." (1 Corinthians 13:4,7)

Discussion prompt: "What does it mean to you to father with love? How do you express love to your children in ways that are meaningful to them?"

Key Teaching Point 3: Integrating Faith and Love in Daily Fathering (10 minutes)
Explain how faith and love work together:

- Faith provides the "why" behind our fathering decisions
- Love determines the "how" of our implementation
- Faith gives us vision of who our children can become
- Love gives us patience with who they are now
- Provide practical examples of faith and love in action:
- Praying with and for your children
- Apologizing when you fall short
- Maintaining consistent discipline with a loving approach
- Sharing your own faith journey authentically

Personal example: Share a brief story of how faith and love guided you through a challenging fatherhood situation.

Discussion prompt: "How might growing in faith and love transform your most challenging parenting situations?"

Small Group Application Exercise (10 minutes)

- Divide into groups of 3-4.
- Have each person share: "What is one specific way you could demonstrate love more effectively to each of your children this week?"
- Encourage group members to consider each child's unique personality and love language in their suggestions.

Next Steps & Assignment Overview (5 minutes)

- Review the reading assignment for next week:
  - Fathering Strong – God's Blueprint for Leading Your Family: Part 2 and Chapters 7-8

- ➤ Explain that next week begins the practical application section focusing on the six core strengths of fatherhood.
- ➤ Encourage them to:
  - ○ Begin identifying specific SMART goals for strengthening their fatherhood journey
  - ○ Practice one new way to demonstrate love to each family member this week
  - ○ Close with a prayer focusing on growing in faith and love as fathers.

Closing Prayer

Loving Father,

We come before You with humble hearts, recognizing that You are the perfect model of fatherhood. Thank You for Your endless patience, boundless love, and faithful presence in our lives.

Lord, as we seek to grow as fathers, deepen our faith so that it becomes the foundation of our parenting. Help us to lead our families not just with our words but through consistent, loving actions that reflect Your character.

Father, we confess the times we've allowed frustration, busyness, or selfishness to overshadow love in our homes. Transform our hearts to love as You love—sacrificially, unconditionally, and wisely. Give us discernment to know when to extend grace and when to hold firm boundaries, always with a spirit of gentleness.

As we leave today, empower us to be intentional in demonstrating love to each of our children in ways that speak directly to their hearts. May they see in us a reflection of Your faithful love that never gives up, never loses faith, is always hopeful, and endures through every circumstance.

Unite us as brothers committed to the sacred calling of fatherhood, supporting and encouraging one another on this journey.

In the name of Jesus, who perfectly embodied both truth and love, Amen.

Facilitation Notes and Tips

For the Welcome & Check-in: As you reach this midpoint in the first third of the workshop, acknowledge both the progress made and the journey ahead. This helps maintain momentum and commitment.

For the Review of Previous Week's Assignment: Listen for how participants are integrating concepts from previous weeks. Make connections between courage/fortitude and this week's focus on faith/love when appropriate.

For the Core Teaching: When discussing faith, be sensitive to participants who may be at different points in their spiritual journey. Focus on practical applications rather than theological depth.

For the love section, emphasize that love in fatherhood often means making difficult decisions. It's not just about being liked by your children but about doing what's best for them.

For the Small Group Exercise: If participants struggle with identifying ways to demonstrate love, suggest they consider their child's interests, personality, and preferred ways of receiving love (words, time, gifts, service, physical affection).

For the Next Steps: Explain that SMART goals (Specific, Measurable, Achievable, Relevant, Time-bound) will be covered more thoroughly in later sessions, but they can begin thinking about concrete, actionable steps for growth.

Potential Challenges and Solutions

Challenge: Participant expresses doubt about the relevance of faith to practical fatherhood.
Solution: Acknowledge their perspective respectfully. Offer practical examples of how faith principles translate to effective fathering regardless of spiritual commitment level. Focus on the practical benefits rather than theological arguments.

Challenge: Discussion reveals significant differences in how participants express love based on their family backgrounds.
Solution: Affirm that there are many valid ways to express love. Redirect to the core principles while acknowledging cultural and family differences: "The expression may look different across families, but the principles of sacrificial, consistent love remain the same."

Challenge: Participant shares that they struggle to love a particularly difficult child.
Solution: Normalize this challenge without minimizing it: "Many fathers find it harder to connect with certain children at certain stages. This doesn't make you a bad father." Suggest practical steps while emphasizing that love is a choice and practice, not just a feeling.

Week 5: Physical Health – Fueling Your Body and Mind

Session Preparation

Room Setup: Same as previous weeks, with seating arranged to facilitate conversation.

Materials Needed:
- Participant Workbooks
- Whiteboard or flip chart
- Markers
- Optional: Simple visual aids showing the connection between physical health and fatherhood effectiveness

Pre-Session Checklist:
- Pray for the session and participants
- Review teaching content and discussion questions
- Prepare personal examples that illustrate key points
- Set up room and any technology

Session Outline (60 minutes)

Welcome & Check-in (5 minutes)
- Warmly welcome everyone back.
- Brief check-in: "Share one way you intentionally demonstrated love to a family member this past week."
- Transition to today's focus on physical health as a foundation for effective fatherhood.

Review of Previous Week's Assignment (10 minutes)
- Ask: "What insights about faith and love stood out to you from the reading?"
- Invite 2-3 participants to share initial thoughts on their SMART goals for fatherhood.
- Address any questions that arose from the reading.

Core Teaching & Discussion (30 minutes)

Key Teaching Point 1: The Lifegevity Approach to Physical Health (10 minutes)
Introduce the Lifegevity concept: balanced physical health that supports longevity and quality of life.
- Explain the three core components:
  - Exercise: Building strength, endurance, and flexibility
  - Nutrition: Fueling your body with appropriate foods
  - Relaxation: Managing stress and ensuring adequate rest
- Discuss how physical health impacts fatherhood:
  - Energy levels for engaging with children
  - Emotional regulation and patience
  - Modeling healthy habits for your family
  - Longevity to be present for important life milestones

Scripture focus: "Do you not know that your bodies are temples of the Holy Spirit, who is in you, whom you have received from God? You are not your own; you were bought at a price. Therefore, honor God with your bodies." (1 Corinthians 6:19-20)

Discussion prompt: "How would you rate your current physical health? What impact does your physical condition have on your effectiveness as a father?"

Key Teaching Point 2: Practical Fitness for Busy Fathers (10 minutes)
Acknowledge the reality of time constraints for most fathers.

Present practical approaches to fitness:

- Finding exercise that fits your lifestyle and preferences
- Incorporating movement throughout your day
- Involving your children in physical activities
- Starting with small, sustainable changes
- Emphasize that the goal is progress, not perfection.

Personal example: Share a brief story about how you've managed physical health amid the demands of fatherhood and work.

Discussion prompt: "What are your biggest challenges when it comes to maintaining physical fitness, and what strategies might help you overcome them?"

Key Teaching Point 3: Nutrition, Rest, and Stress Management (10 minutes)

- Provide practical nutritional guidance:
  - Focus on whole foods when possible
  - Mindful eating rather than restrictive dieting
  - Hydration as a foundation for health
  - Moderation rather than elimination of enjoyable foods
- Discuss the importance of adequate rest:
  - Sleep as a non-negotiable health factor
  - The connection between sleep and emotional regulation
  - Strategies for improving sleep quality
- Address stress management techniques:
  - Brief mindfulness practices
  - Physical activity as stress relief
  - Setting appropriate boundaries
  - The role of prayer and spiritual practices

Discussion prompt: "What one change to your nutrition, sleep, or stress management would make the biggest positive impact on your fatherhood?"

Small Group Application Exercise (10 minutes)

- Divide into groups of 3-4.
- Have each person identify:
  - One realistic physical health goal for the coming month
  - Potential obstacles to achieving that goal
  - Strategies for overcoming those obstacles

o   Group members offer support and additional suggestions.

Next Steps & Assignment Overview (5 minutes)

➢ Review the reading assignment for next week:
  o   Fathering Strong – God's Blueprint for Leading Your Family: Chapter 9
  o   Fathering Strong – 30-Day Devotional and Journal: Complete Day 3 of the 7-Day Awakening
➢ Encourage them to develop 2-3 SMART goals for improving their physical health in support of their fatherhood.
➢ Remind them that physical health goals should be realistic and sustainable, focusing on progress rather than perfection.
➢ Close with a prayer for wisdom and discipline in caring for their physical health.

Closing Prayer

Heavenly Father,

We thank You for the bodies You've given us—temples that house Your Spirit and provide the strength and energy we need to serve our families well.

Lord, grant us wisdom to make choices that honor these bodies You've entrusted to us. Help us recognize that caring for our physical health isn't about vanity but about stewardship that enables us to be present, engaged, and energetic fathers.

Father, we ask for discipline in areas where we struggle—whether it's making better food choices, prioritizing rest, managing stress, or being more active. Remove the obstacles of excuses, procrastination, and discouragement that so often derail our good intentions.

Give us balance, Lord. Show us how to model healthy habits without making them idols how to pursue wellness without neglecting our families in the process.

We pray for Your strength when our resolve weakens, for community to support our efforts, and for grace when we fall short. Help us remember that small, consistent steps forward matter more than perfection.

May our commitment to physical health ultimately serve Your purpose: equipping us to love and lead our families with endurance, clarity, and joy for the long journey of fatherhood.

In Jesus' name, Amen.

Facilitation Notes and Tips

For the Welcome & Check-in: Be prepared for some participants to express discomfort with the topic of physical health. Acknowledge that this can be a sensitive area for many men.

For the Review of Previous Week's Assignment: Listen for how participants are beginning to integrate concepts from previous weeks into a cohesive approach to fatherhood.

For the Core Teaching: Emphasize that physical health is about stewardship of the body God has given, not about achieving a certain look or comparing oneself to others.

Be sensitive to potential health conditions or limitations that participants may have. Always include modifications and emphasize that each person's health journey is unique.

Avoid prescriptive, one-size-fits-all approaches to diet and exercise. Focus on principles that can be adapted to individual circumstances.

For the Small Group Exercise: If participants struggle to identify realistic goals, suggest starting points: drinking more water, taking a daily walk, going to bed 30 minutes earlier, etc.

For the Next Steps: Remind participants that physical health goals should support their fatherhood, not compete with it. The time invested should enhance their energy and capacity for family engagement.

Potential Challenges and Solutions

Challenge: Participant expresses that they have no time for physical health with work and family demands.
Solution: Acknowledge the real challenge of time constraints. Suggest integration rather than addition: "How might you incorporate movement while spending time with your children? What small nutritional changes require minimal time investment?"

Challenge: Participant has significant health issues that limit traditional exercise approaches.
Solution: Affirm that health looks different for everyone: "The goal is to optimize your health within your unique circumstances. What forms of movement are accessible and beneficial for you? Let's focus on what you can do rather than what you can't."

Challenge: Group dynamic shifts to competitive comparison of fitness levels.
Solution: Gently redirect: "Remember, our physical health goals are about becoming better fathers, not competing with each other. Each of us has different starting points and challenges."

Week 6: Spiritual Health – Connecting to the True Father

Session Preparation

Room Setup: Same as previous weeks, with seating arranged to facilitate conversation.

Materials Needed:
- Participant Workbooks
- Whiteboard or flip chart
- Markers
- Optional: Visual aid showing the connection between spiritual disciplines and fatherhood

Pre-Session Checklist:
- Pray for the session and participants
- Review teaching content and discussion questions
- Prepare personal examples that illustrate key points
- Set up room and any technology

Session Outline (60 minutes)

Welcome & Check-in (5 minutes)
- Warmly welcome everyone back.
- Brief check-in: "Share one step you took toward better physical health this past week."
- Transition to today's focus on spiritual health as the core of effective fatherhood.

Review of Previous Week's Assignment (10 minutes)
- Ask: "What insights about physical health and fatherhood stood out to you from the reading?"
- Invite 2-3 participants to share their SMART goals for physical health.
- Address any questions that arose from the reading or Day 3 of the devotional.

Core Teaching & Discussion (30 minutes)

Key Teaching Point 1: The Father-Son Relationship with God (10 minutes)

Explain how our relationship with God as Father forms the foundation for our own fathering:
- We can only give what we have received
- Our view of God shapes our fathering approach
- Regular connection with God provides wisdom beyond our own
- Spiritual health fuels emotional resilience in fatherhood challenges
- Discuss the difference between religious activity and authentic relationship with God.

Scripture focus: "Yet to all who did receive him, to those who believed in his name, he gave the right to become children of God." (John 1:12)

Discussion prompt: "How would you describe your current relationship with God as Father? How does this relationship influence your own fathering?"

Key Teaching Point 2: Core Spiritual Disciplines for Fathers (10 minutes)

Present practical spiritual disciplines that strengthen fatherhood:

➢ **Prayer:** Both structured and conversational approaches

➢ **Scripture engagement:** Finding Wisdom for family leadership

➢ **Worship:** Maintaining proper perspective on challenges

➢ **Community:** The support of other believing fathers

➢ **Service:** Modeling selflessness for your children

➢ Emphasize starting with manageable practices rather than overwhelming commitments.

Personal example: Share briefly how a specific spiritual discipline has strengthened your fatherhood.

Discussion prompt: "Which spiritual discipline currently provides the most strength for your fatherhood? Which one would you like to develop further?"

Key Teaching Point 3: Integrating Spiritual Leadership in Your Home (10 minutes)

Discuss practical approaches to spiritual leadership:

➢ Age-appropriate faith conversations with children

➢ Incorporating faith naturally into daily routines

➢ Modeling authentic faith rather than perfection

➢ Creating family traditions that reinforce values

➢ Responding to children's spiritual questions honestly

Address common challenges:

➢ Feeling inadequate as a spiritual leader

➢ Resistance from family members

➢ Inconsistency in personal practices

➢ Balancing teaching with allowing children to develop their own faith

Scripture focus: "These commandments that I give you today are to be on your hearts. Impress them on your children. Talk about them when you sit at home and when you walk along the road when you lie down, and when you get up." (Deuteronomy 6:6-7)

Discussion prompt: "What is one practical way you could strengthen spiritual leadership in your home this week?"

Small Group Application Exercise (10 minutes)

➢ Divide into groups of 3-4.

➢ Have each person identify:

➢ Their current strongest spiritual discipline

➢ One spiritual practice they want to develop or strengthen

➢ A specific, realistic step toward that growth

➢ Group members offer encouragement and accountability suggestions.

Next Steps & Assignment Overview (5 minutes)

➢ Review the reading assignment for next week:

o Fathering Strong – God's Blueprint for Leading Your Family: Chapter 10

- Fathering Strong – 30-Day Devotional and Journal: Complete Day 4 of the 7-Day Awakening

➤ Encourage them to:
- Develop 1-2 SMART goals for spiritual growth that will strengthen their fatherhood
- Identify one way to more intentionally lead spiritually in their home this week
- Close with a prayer for deepening relationship with God as Father and for wisdom in spiritual leadership.

Closing Prayer

Heavenly Father,

We come before You with grateful hearts, recognizing that all fatherhood flows from You. Thank You for the perfect example of fatherhood You provide—patient, present, wise, and unfailingly loving.

Lord, deepen our relationship with You as our Father. Help us experience Your love more fully so we can reflect it more clearly to our children. Where our understanding of fatherhood has been wounded by earthly experiences, bring healing and restoration.

Grant us wisdom as spiritual leaders in our homes. Show us how to create rhythms of faith that feel authentic rather than forced. Give us discernment to know when to speak and when to listen, when to teach, and when to simply model faith through our actions.

Father, we confess the times we've abdicated our spiritual responsibility or approached it halfheartedly. Renew our vision for the eternal impact of spiritual leadership. Help us see beyond the daily resistance or apparent indifference we might encounter.

Equip us with courage to lead even when we feel inadequate, with consistency when we're tempted to give up, and with humility to acknowledge our own need for growth.

May our children see in us men who genuinely seek after Your heart—not perfect men, but authentic followers committed to the journey of faith.

We ask this in the name of Jesus, who showed us the way to You, Amen.

Facilitation Notes and Tips

For the Welcome & Check-in: Be sensitive to varying levels of spiritual maturity and commitment among participants. Create an atmosphere of acceptance rather than judgment.

For the Review of Previous Week's Assignment: Note connections between physical and spiritual health when participants share. Highlight how these areas of strength work together.

For the Core Teaching: When discussing relationships with God as Father, be aware that some participants may have had difficult relationships with their earthly fathers, affecting their view of God. Acknowledge this reality when appropriate.

Present spiritual disciplines as life-giving practices rather than burdensome obligations. Emphasize grace over legalism.

For the Small Group Exercise: If participants struggle to identify spiritual practices, offer simple starting points: a five-minute morning prayer time, reading one chapter of Proverbs daily, or listening to worship music during commutes.

For the Next Steps: Remind participants that spiritual leadership is more about authenticity than perfection. Children benefit more from seeing their fathers genuinely pursuing God than from a flawless performance.

Potential Challenges and Solutions

Challenge: Participant expresses feeling inadequate as a spiritual leader due to past failures or limited biblical knowledge.

Solution: Affirm that spiritual leadership begins with authenticity: "Your children need to see you genuinely pursuing God, not perfectly understanding everything. Start where you are, be honest about your journey, and grow alongside them."

Challenge: Participant shares resistance from spouse or children to spiritual leadership attempts.

Solution: Suggest a gentle, consistent approach: "Spiritual influence often comes through loving example before teaching. How might you demonstrate your faith values through actions that bless your family, creating openness to more direct spiritual conversations?"

Challenge: Significant differences in spiritual commitment levels emerge among participants.

Solution: Maintain an inclusive approach: "Each of us is on a journey with God. Today's discussion is about taking your next step, whatever that looks like for you personally."

Week 7: Emotional Wealth – Mastering Your Inner World

Session Preparation

Room Setup: Same as previous weeks, with seating arranged to facilitate conversation.

Materials Needed:

➤ Participant Workbooks

➤ Whiteboard or flip chart

➤ Markers

➤ Optional: Visual aid showing the connection between emotional health and effective fatherhood

Pre-Session Checklist:

➤ Pray for the session and participants

➤ Review teaching content and discussion questions

➤ Prepare personal examples that illustrate key points

➤ Set up room and any technology

Session Outline (60 minutes)

Welcome & Check-in (5 minutes)

➤ Warmly welcome everyone back.

➤ Brief check-in: "Share one way you practiced spiritual leadership in your home this past week."

➤ Transition to today's focus on emotional wealth and its critical importance to fatherhood.

Review of Previous Week's Assignment (10 minutes)

➤ Ask: "What insights about spiritual health and fatherhood stood out to you from the reading?"

➤ Invite 2-3 participants to share their SMART goals for spiritual growth.

➤ Address any questions that arose from the reading or Day 4 of the devotional.

Core Teaching & Discussion (30 minutes)

Key Teaching Point 1: Understanding Emotional Wealth (10 minutes)

Define emotional wealth as the ability to:

➤ Identify and name your emotions accurately

➤ Regulate emotional responses appropriately

➤ Demonstrate emotional presence with your children

➤ Model healthy emotional expression for your family

Explain how emotional health impacts fatherhood:

- ➢ Ability to respond rather than react to challenging behavior
- ➢ Capacity to create emotional safety for children
- ➢ Effectiveness in disciplining without anger or harshness
- ➢ Modeling emotional intelligence for your children

Scripture focus: "The fruit of the Spirit is love, joy, peace, forbearance, kindness, goodness, faithfulness, gentleness and self-control." (Galatians 5:22-23)

Discussion prompt: "How would you assess your current emotional wealth as a father? In what situations do you find emotional regulation most challenging?"

Key Teaching Point 2: Breaking Unhealthy Emotional Patterns (10 minutes)

Discuss common emotional challenges fathers face:

- ➢ Suppressing emotions rather than processing them
- ➢ Expressing only "acceptable" emotions like anger while hiding vulnerability
- ➢ Replicating unhealthy patterns from their own upbringing
- ➢ Using work or activities to avoid emotional engagement

Present a framework for emotional growth:

- ➢ **Awareness:** Recognizing emotional triggers and patterns
- ➢ **Acceptance:** Acknowledging emotions without judgment
- ➢ **Action:** Choosing healthier responses to emotional situations

Personal example: Share briefly about overcoming an unhealthy emotional pattern in your own fatherhood journey.

Discussion prompt: "What unhealthy emotional pattern from your past or present would you most like to change in your fatherhood?"

Key Teaching Point 3: Practical Tools for Emotional Mastery (10 minutes)

Provide specific strategies for developing emotional wealth:

- ➢ **The pause principle:** Creating space between trigger and response
- ➢ **Emotional vocabulary:** Expanding the ability to name feelings precisely
- ➢ **Stress management techniques:** Physical activity, deep breathing, mindfulness
- ➢ **Healthy emotional expression:** Appropriate vulnerability with children
- ➢ **Seeking support:** The role of mentors, friends, and professional help when needed

Emphasize the connection between spiritual disciplines and emotional regulation.

Scripture focus: "Everyone should be quick to listen, slow to speak and slow to become angry because human anger does not produce the righteousness that God desires." (James 1:19-20)

Discussion prompt: "Which of these emotional mastery tools do you most need to develop, and how might it transform your fatherhood?"

Small Group Application Exercise (10 minutes)

Divide into groups of 3-4.

Have each person identify:

- ➢ A specific situation that consistently triggers difficult emotions
- ➢ The typical emotional response and its impact on their family

> ➤ One strategy they could implement for a healthier response
> ➤ Group members offer supportive feedback and additional suggestions.

Next Steps & Assignment Overview (5 minutes)

Review the reading assignment for next week:

> ➤ Fathering Strong – God's Blueprint for Leading Your Family: Chapter 11
> ➤ Fathering Strong – 30-Day Devotional and Journal: Complete Day 5 of the 7-Day Awakening

Encourage them to:

> ➤ Develop 1-2 SMART Develop 1-2 SMART goals for emotional growth that will strengthen their fatherhood
> ➤ Practice the pause principle in at least one triggering situation this week
> ➤ Begin noticing emotional patterns and their impact on family interactions
> ➤ Close with a prayer for emotional wisdom, healing from past wounds, and the courage to model healthy emotional expression for their children.

Closing Prayer

Heavenly Father,

We come before You today, acknowledging that our emotions are a gift from You, yet sometimes they become barriers in our relationships with our children and families. Lord, we ask for Your wisdom to navigate our emotional landscapes with grace and intention.

Grant us discernment to recognize the emotional patterns that have been passed down through generations. Where there are wounds from our own fathers or childhood experiences, we ask for Your healing touch. Transform those places of pain into wisdom that can guide our children.

Father, give us courage to be emotionally honest—to model for our children what healthy emotional expression looks like. Help us demonstrate that strength isn't found in hiding our feelings but in expressing them appropriately and using them to connect rather than divide.

When we feel overwhelmed, teach us to pause and seek Your perspective before responding. When anger rises, remind us of Your patience. When fear threatens to control our decisions, fill us with Your perfect love that casts out fear.

Lord, we desire to leave an emotional legacy that reflects Your heart. May our children learn from watching us that it's possible to be both strong and tender, both truthful and kind.

In Jesus' name, we pray, Amen.

Facilitation Notes and Tips

For the Welcome & Check-in: Be prepared for varying levels of comfort when discussing emotions. Some men may initially use humor or intellectualization to avoid emotional vulnerability.

For the Review of Previous Week's Assignment: Listen for connections between spiritual practices and emotional regulation that participants may have noticed during the week.

For the Core Teaching: When discussing emotional patterns, acknowledge that many men were raised with limited emotional expression models. Create a safe space that normalizes the challenges of emotional growth.

Balance validation of struggle with encouragement toward growth. Avoid both minimizing emotional challenges and dwelling exclusively on difficulties.

For the Small Group Exercise: If participants struggle to identify emotional triggers, suggest common scenarios: child misbehavior in public, feeling disrespected, work stress affecting home life, or comparison with other fathers.

For the Next Steps: Emphasize that emotional growth is a process that requires patience and practice. Small, consistent changes lead to significant transformation over time.

Potential Challenges and Solutions

Challenge: Participant expresses belief that emotional control means suppressing all feelings.
Solution: Clarify the difference between suppression and regulation: "Emotional wealth isn't about not feeling; it's about feeling appropriately and expressing emotions in healthy ways. Strong fathers aren't emotionless—they're emotionally wise."

Challenge: Group becomes uncomfortable with emotional vulnerability.
Solution: Model appropriate vulnerability while maintaining leadership presence. Acknowledge: "These conversations can feel uncomfortable because many of us weren't taught to discuss emotions openly. That discomfort is normal and worth pushing through for our families' benefit."

Challenge: Participant reveals significant emotional trauma requiring professional support.
Solution: Affirm their courage in sharing while suggesting additional resources: "Thank you for trusting us with that experience. That kind of pain often benefits from professional support alongside what we're learning here. I'd be happy to suggest some resources after our session."

Week 8: Financial Wisdom – Stewarding God's Resources as a Father

Session Preparation

Room Setup: Same as previous weeks, with seating arranged to facilitate conversation.

Materials Needed:

- Participant Workbooks
- Whiteboard or flip chart
- Markers
- Optional: Simple visual aids showing biblical financial principles

Pre-Session Checklist:

- Pray for the session and participants
- Review teaching content and discussion questions
- Prepare personal examples that illustrate key points
- Set up room and any technology

Session Outline (60 minutes)

Welcome & Check-in (5 minutes)

- Warmly welcome everyone back.
- Brief check-in: "Share one situation this past week where you practiced emotional awareness or regulation."
- Transition to today's focus on financial wisdom as a critical component of effective fatherhood.

Review of Previous Week's Assignment (10 minutes)

- Ask: "What insights about emotional wealth stood out to you from the reading?"
- Invite 2-3 participants to share their SMART goals for emotional growth.
- Address any questions that arose from the reading or Day 5 of the devotional.

Core Teaching & Discussion (30 minutes)

Key Teaching Point 1: Biblical Foundations of Financial Stewardship (10 minutes)

Establish the biblical perspective on finances:

- God owns everything; we are managers, not owners
- Financial decisions reflect and shape our values
- Generosity as a spiritual discipline
- The connection between financial health and family stability

Discuss how financial wisdom impacts fatherhood:

- Providing for family needs
- Teaching children biblical money principles
- Creating a margin for generosity and opportunity

> ➤ Reducing stress that affects family relationships

Scripture focus: "For where your treasure is, there your heart will be also." (Matthew 6:21)

Discussion prompt: "How do your financial habits currently align with your values as a father? Where do you see disconnects?"

Key Teaching Point 2: Core Financial Principles for Fathers (10 minutes)

Present practical financial wisdom:

> ➤ Budgeting as a Family Values Statement
> ➤ Debt management and the path to financial freedom
> ➤ Saving and investing for family needs and goals
> ➤ Giving as a family practice
> ➤ Teaching children age-appropriate financial responsibility
> ➤ Emphasize that financial wisdom is about stewardship, not accumulation.

Personal example: Share briefly about implementing a financial principle that strengthened your family.

Discussion prompt: "Which financial principle do you find most challenging to implement, and why?"

Key Teaching Point 3: Creating a Family Financial Vision (10 minutes)

Guide participants in developing a family financial approach:

> ➤ Identifying core financial values to pass to children
> ➤ Having healthy financial conversations with your spouse
> ➤ Setting short and long-term family financial goals
> ➤ Creating teaching moments about money with children
> ➤ Balancing provision with avoiding materialism

Address common challenges:

> ➤ Financial disagreements with spouse
> ➤ Cultural pressure for material accumulation
> ➤ Teaching contentment in a consumer society
> ➤ Balancing work demands with family presence

Scripture focus: "Keep your lives free from the love of money and be content with what you have, because God has said, 'Never will I leave you; never will I forsake you.'" (Hebrews 13:5)

Discussion prompt: "What is one financial habit or practice you want your children to develop, and how can you model it more effectively?"

Small Group Application Exercise (10 minutes)

Divide into groups of 3-4.

Have each person identify:

> ➤ One financial strength in their current approach
> ➤ One financial area needing improvement
> ➤ A specific step they could take toward better financial stewardship
> ➤ Group members offer supportive feedback and additional suggestions.

Next Steps & Assignment Overview (5 minutes)

Review the reading assignment for next week:

> ➤ Fathering Strong – God's Blueprint for Leading Your Family: Chapter 12
> ➤ Fathering Strong – 30-Day Devotional and Journal: Complete Day 6 of the 7-Day Awakening

Encourage them to:

> ➤ Develop 1-2 SMART goals for financial stewardship
> ➤ Have one intentional conversation about money with their spouse or children
> ➤ Consider one area where greater financial margin would strengthen their fatherhood

Close with a prayer for wisdom in managing resources, contentment with God's provision, and clarity about financial priorities that honor God and serve their families.

Closing Prayer

Heavenly Father,

We come before You with grateful hearts, recognizing that everything we have comes from Your generous hand. As fathers seeking to lead our families with wisdom, we ask for Your guidance in managing the resources You've entrusted to us.

Lord, in a world that constantly tells us we need more, plant within us a deep contentment with what You have provided. Help us find joy not in possessions but in Your presence, remembering Your promise that You will never leave us nor forsake us.

Grant us wisdom to make financial decisions that honor You—choices that demonstrate good stewardship, generosity, and faith. Show us how to model these principles for our children, teaching them through both our words and actions that our security rests in You, not in earthly wealth.

Father, give us clarity about financial priorities that truly matter. Help us distinguish between wants and needs, between temporary satisfaction and lasting value. Where we've developed unhealthy patterns or attitudes about money, transform our thinking to align with Your truth.

May our financial choices create a margin that strengthens our families and allows us to serve others. Let our children see in us men who handle money with integrity, generosity, and eternal perspective.

In Jesus' name, we pray, Amen.

Facilitation Notes and Tips

For the Welcome & Check-in: Recognize that financial discussions can trigger various emotions based on participants' backgrounds and current situations. Create an atmosphere that acknowledges different financial starting points without judgment.

For the Review of Previous Week's Assignment: Listen for connections participants may make between emotional regulation and financial decision-making, as these areas often influence each other.

For the Core Teaching: When discussing biblical financial principles, focus on stewardship rather than specific financial achievements. Emphasize that financial wisdom is about faithfulness with whatever resources God has provided.

Present financial principles in ways that apply to various income levels. Avoid assumptions about participants' financial situations or access to financial tools.

For the Small Group Exercise: If participants seem reluctant to discuss finances specifically, encourage them to focus on the values and principles they want to model rather than dollar amounts.

For the Next Steps: Remind participants that financial transformation, like other areas of growth, happens through consistent small changes rather than dramatic overhauls.

Potential Challenges and Solutions

Challenge: Significant financial disparity among participants creates discomfort.
Solution: Emphasize principles over specifics: "Financial wisdom operates on the same principles regardless of income level. Today, we're focusing on stewardship and values, not specific financial targets."

Challenge: Participant expresses shame or embarrassment about financial struggles.
Solution: Normalize the journey while encouraging growth: "Many of us have financial regrets or challenges. The question isn't where we've been, but what next step will move us toward better stewardship."

Challenge: Participant questions whether certain financial practices are truly biblical.
Solution: Focus on core principles while acknowledging room for different applications: "Scripture gives us clear principles about generosity, diligence, and avoiding the love of money, while leaving room for different practical applications of those principles."

Week 9: A Strong Marriage - The Foundation of the Family

Session Preparation

Room Setup: Same as previous weeks, with seating arranged to facilitate conversation.

Materials Needed:

➤ Participant Workbooks
➤ Whiteboard or flip chart
➤ Markers
➤ Optional: Marriage covenant visual aid
➤ Optional: Photos showing family systems (can be stock photos)

Pre-Session Checklist:

➤ Pray for the session and participants
➤ Review teaching content and discussion questions
➤ Prepare personal examples that illustrate key points
➤ Set up room and any technology

Session Outline (60 minutes)

Welcome & Check-in (5 minutes)

➤ Warmly welcome everyone back.
➤ Brief check-in: "Share one financial principle you've started implementing since our last meeting."
➤ Transition to today's focus on marriage as the foundation for effective fatherhood.

Review of Previous Week's Assignment (10 minutes)

➤ Ask: "What challenges or victories did you experience in applying financial wisdom principles this week?"
➤ Invite 2-3 participants to share their financial stewardship goals and initial steps taken.
➤ Address any questions that arose from the reading or Day 6 of the devotional.

Core Teaching & Discussion (30 minutes)

Key Teaching Point 1: The Biblical Design for Marriage (10 minutes)

➤ Marriage as a covenant relationship, not just a contract
➤ How a healthy marriage provides security and stability for children
➤ The father's role in honoring and supporting his wife

Discussion Questions:

How does the quality of your marriage affect your effectiveness as a father?

What did you learn about marriage from your own parents? How has that influenced your approach?

Key Teaching Point 2: Communication and Conflict Resolution (10 minutes)

➢ Healthy communication patterns that children observe and internalize

➢ Resolving conflicts in ways that model respect and reconciliation

➢ The importance of unity in parenting decisions

Discussion Questions:

What communication patterns do you want your children to learn from observing your marriage?

How do you and your spouse handle disagreements about parenting approaches?

Key Teaching Point 3: Prioritizing Your Marriage While Parenting (10 minutes)

➢ Practical ways to maintain connection with your spouse amid parenting demands

➢ How investing in your marriage benefits your children

➢ Balancing marriage and parenting responsibilities

Discussion Questions:

What practical steps do you take to keep your marriage strong while raising children?

How do you demonstrate to your children that your marriage is a priority?

Small Group Exercise (10 minutes)

In groups of 3-4, discuss:

➢ One specific way you can strengthen your marriage this week

➢ How this action might positively impact your children

➢ If single or widowed, discuss how you can model healthy relationships and respect for your children's mother

Next Steps & Assignment (5 minutes)

Review the reading assignment for next week:

➢ Fathering Strong – God's Blueprint for Leading Your Family: Chapter 13

➢ Fathering Strong – 30-Day Devotional and Journal: Complete Day 7 of the 7-Day Awakening

Encourage them to:

➢ Schedule a dedicated time with your spouse this week to discuss your marriage and parenting partnership

➢ For single fathers: Reflect on how to speak respectfully about your children's mother and model healthy relationships

➢ Develop 1-2 SMART goals for strengthening your marriage or co-parenting relationship

Closing (5 minutes)

➢ Summarize key points about marriage as the foundation for effective fatherhood

➢ Remind participants: "Your marriage is the most important human relationship in your home. As you nurture it, you create the secure foundation your children need."

➢ Close in prayer, asking for wisdom and strength in both marriage and fatherhood

Closing Prayer

Heavenly Father,

We come before You with humble hearts, recognizing that strong marriages and effective fatherhood require Your wisdom and strength daily. Thank You for the gift of marriage that serves as the foundation for our families.

Lord, we ask for Your guidance in our marriages. Help us to love our spouses as Christ loved the church—sacrificially and unconditionally. Where there is hurt, bring healing; where there is distance, restore connection; where there is weariness, renew strength.

For those of us parenting alone or co-parenting across households, grant us grace and wisdom to honor the mothers of our children and model respectful relationships.

Father, equip us to lead our families with both strength and tenderness. When we falter, remind us that Your power is made perfect in our weakness. Help us create homes where our children feel secure in the knowledge that their parents' relationship is built on love, respect, and commitment.

Give us discernment to know when to speak and when to listen, when to stand firm and when to extend grace—both in our marriages and in our parenting.

May our children witness in us men who prioritize their marriages and parent with intention, not perfect men, but faithful men committed to growth.

We ask this in Jesus' name, Amen.

Facilitator Notes and Tips

Be sensitive to single fathers, widowers, or those in struggling marriages. Adapt language to be inclusive while maintaining the importance of the marriage relationship.

Use personal examples judiciously, respecting your own spouse's privacy.

Emphasize that strengthening marriage is a journey, not a destination.

For the Discussion: Encourage vulnerability but maintain appropriate boundaries. If marital issues arise that need professional help, have resources ready to recommend.

For the Small Group Exercise: If participants seem reluctant to discuss marriage specifically, provide prompts about general relationship principles they want to model for their children.

For the Next Steps: Emphasize that small, consistent investments in marriage yield significant returns in family health.

Potential Challenges and Solutions

Challenge: Participant in a troubled marriage feels discouraged or defensive.
Solution: Acknowledge that all marriages face seasons of challenge while offering hope: "Every marriage has growth areas. Today's focus is on taking one step forward, not achieving perfection."

Challenge: Single father feels excluded from the conversation.
Solution: Broaden the discussion: "The principles of respect, communication, and honor apply to co-parenting relationships as well, even when you're not married."

Challenge: Participant dominates discussion with marital complaints.
Solution: Redirect gently: "Those are real challenges. For our purposes today, let's focus on the positive steps we can take rather than the problems we face."

Week 10: Building Lasting Bonds with Your Children

Session Preparation

Room Setup: Same as previous weeks, with seating arranged to facilitate conversation.

Materials Needed:

- Participant Workbooks
- Whiteboard or flip chart
- Markers
- Optional: Visual aid showing different stages of child development
- Optional: Photos illustrating father-child bonding activities

Pre-Session Checklist:

- Pray for the session and participants
- Review teaching content and discussion questions
- Prepare personal examples that illustrate key points
- Set up room and any technology

Session Outline (60 minutes)

Welcome & Check-in (5 minutes)

- Warmly welcome everyone back.
- Brief check-in: "Share one way you invested in your marriage or co-parenting relationship this past week."
- Transition to today's focus on building deep, lasting bonds with your children.

Review of Previous Week's Assignment (10 minutes)

- Ask: "What insights about marriage and fatherhood stood out to you from the reading?"
- Invite 2-3 participants to share their SMART goals for strengthening their marriage or co-parenting relationship.
- Address any questions that arose from the reading or Day 7 of the devotional.

Core Teaching & Discussion (30 minutes)

Key Teaching Point 1: Understanding Your Child's Unique Design (10 minutes)

Discuss how to recognize and nurture each child's individuality:

- Observing your child's temperament, interests, and gifts
- Adapting your parenting approach to each child's needs
- The difference between treating children equally versus uniquely
- How to affirm your child's God-given design

Scripture focus: "For you created my inmost being; you knit me together in my mother's womb. I praise you because I am fearfully and wonderfully made." (Psalm 139:13-14)

Discussion prompt: "How are your children different from each other, and how do you adapt your fathering approach to meet their unique needs?"

Key Teaching Point 2: Quality Time and Meaningful Presence (10 minutes)

Present practical approaches to deepening father-child connections:

➤ The power of undivided attention

➤ Creating regular one-on-one time with each child

➤ Engaging in activities that match your child's interests

➤ Building family traditions and rituals

➤ Being fully present, even during brief interactions

➤ Emphasize that consistency matters more than grand gestures.

Personal example: Share briefly about a meaningful connection ritual with your own child.

Discussion prompt: "What activities or moments seem to create the strongest connections with each of your children?"

Key Teaching Point 3: Communication That Builds Trust (10 minutes)

Explain how to develop open, trust-building communication:

➤ Active listening without immediate problem-solving

➤ Age-appropriate vulnerability and authenticity

➤ Creating a safe space for children to express all emotions

➤ Asking questions that invite deeper conversation

➤ Maintaining connection during disciplinary moments

Address common challenges:

➤ Communicating with reluctant or quiet children

➤ Navigating technology distractions

➤ Rebuilding trust after disconnection

➤ Adjusting communication as children grow and mature

Scripture focus: "My dear brothers and sisters, take note of this: Everyone should be quick to listen, slow to speak, and slow to become angry." (James 1:19)

Discussion prompt: "What is your biggest communication challenge with your children, and what might help you overcome it?"

Small Group Application Exercise (10 minutes)

Divide into groups of 3-4.

Have each person identify:

➤ One strength in their current bonding with their children

➤ One area where deeper connection is needed

➤ A specific activity or approach they could implement this week

➤ Group members offer supportive feedback and additional suggestions.

Next Steps & Assignment Overview (5 minutes)

Review the reading assignment for next week:

➤ Fathering Strong – God's Blueprint for Leading Your Family: Chapter 14

➤ Fathering Strong – 30-Day Devotional and Journal: Complete Week 2, Days 8-14

Encourage them to:

- ➢ Schedule one-on-one time with each child in the coming week
- ➢ Develop 1-2 SMART goals for strengthening bonds with their children
- ➢ Begin a new family tradition or ritual that fosters connection
- ➢ Close with a prayer for wisdom in understanding each child's unique design, patience in building trust, and joy in the journey of fatherhood.

Closing Prayer

Heavenly Father,

We stand before You as fathers, each blessed with children of remarkable and unique design. Lord, we thank You for the gift of our children, each one fearfully and wonderfully made by Your hands.

Grant us wisdom, Father, to see beyond surface behaviors to the hearts You have crafted. Help us recognize and celebrate the distinct personalities, gifts, and needs of each child You've entrusted to us. Where we have tried to shape them in our own image rather than discovering Your design, forgive us and redirect our paths.

Lord, we ask for patience as we build trust with our children. In moments of frustration or misunderstanding, slow our reactions and quicken our listening. Remind us that trust is built in small moments of consistency, in promises kept and presence maintained. Help us remember that the time invested now yields relationships that will sustain through challenges ahead.

Father, in a world that often makes parenting feel heavy with responsibility, restore to us the joy of fatherhood. Help us delight in our children as You delight in us. May we find wonder in watching them grow, laughter in their discoveries, and gratitude in the privilege of guiding them.

As we leave this place, empower us to be the fathers You have called us to be—not perfect, but present; not flawless, but faithful. May our children see in us a reflection of Your perfect love.

In the name of Jesus, our ultimate example of sacrificial love, Amen.

Facilitation Notes and Tips

For the Welcome & Check-in: Recognize that participants may have varying levels of comfort with emotional connection based on their own childhood experiences. Create space that validates different starting points while encouraging growth.

For the Review of Previous Week's Assignment: Listen for how participants are connecting marriage strength to their fathering effectiveness, affirming these insights when shared.

For the Core Teaching: When discussing children's unique design, emphasize that understanding differences isn't about labeling or limiting children but about connecting with them more effectively.

Present bonding strategies that work across different family structures, schedules, and life stages. Acknowledge the challenges of building connection amid busy schedules while offering practical solutions.

For the Small Group Exercise: If participants struggle to identify connection activities, suggest simple options like bedtime rituals, shared hobbies, physical play, or conversation starters during daily routines.

For the Next Steps: Remind participants that relationship-building is cumulative—small, consistent investments yield significant returns over time.

Potential Challenges and Solutions

Challenge: Participant expresses frustration with a child who seems resistant to connection.
Solution: Normalize the challenge while offering hope: "Children go through seasons of connection and independence. Persistence and patience are key—keep offering connection opportunities without pressure, and watch for moments when they're more receptive."

Challenge: Participant reveals significant regret about past disconnection.
Solution: Emphasize the opportunity for repair: "One of the most powerful things about father-child relationships is that it's never too late to begin healing. Children respond remarkably to sincere efforts to connect, even after difficult seasons."

Challenge: Participant struggles to identify unique qualities in their children.
Solution: Offer observation prompts: "Sometimes we discover our children's uniqueness by watching how they approach challenges, what brings them joy, or how they interact with others. This week, try observing your child with fresh eyes as if you're meeting them for the first time."

Week 11: Setting Your Goals and Putting It All Together

Session Preparation

Room Setup: Same as previous weeks, with seating arranged to facilitate conversation.

Materials Needed:

➢ Participant Workbooks

➢ Whiteboard or flip chart

➢ Markers

➢ Printed goal-setting worksheets

➢ Optional: Visual timeline showing the fatherhood journey

Pre-Session Checklist:

➢ Pray for the session and participants

➢ Review teaching content and discussion questions

➢ Prepare personal examples that illustrate key points

➢ Set up room and any technology

Session Outline (60 minutes)

Welcome & Check-in (5 minutes)

➢ Warmly welcome everyone back.

➢ Brief check-in: "Share one meaningful connection moment you had with your child this past week."

➢ Transition to today's focus on integrating all we've learned and creating an actionable fatherhood plan.

Review of Previous Week's Assignment (10 minutes)

➢ Ask: "What insights about building bonds with your children stood out to you from the reading?"

➢ Invite 2-3 participants to share their experiences with one-on-one time with their children.

➢ Address any questions that arose from the reading or Week 2 of the devotional.

Core Teaching & Discussion (30 minutes)

Key Teaching Point 1: The Power of Intentional Fatherhood (10 minutes)

Summarize the journey of the past ten weeks:

➢ The five pillars of strong fatherhood we've explored

➢ The difference between reactive and proactive fatherhood

➢ Why written goals and plans matter for family leadership

➢ How intentionality breaks negative generational patterns

Scripture focus: "But as for me and my household, we will serve the LORD." (Joshua 24:15)

Discussion prompt: "Looking back over our time together, what has been your most significant insight or change in your approach to fatherhood?"

Key Teaching Point 2: Creating Your Fatherhood Vision (10 minutes)

- Guide participants in developing a compelling vision:
- Imagining your relationship with your children in 10-20 years
- Identifying the values and character qualities you want to instill
- Clarifying the spiritual legacy you want to leave
- Considering the memories and experiences you want to create
- Emphasize that a clear vision drives daily decisions and priorities.

Personal example: Share briefly about your own fatherhood vision and how it guides your choices.

Discussion prompt: "If you could fast-forward to your child's wedding day or 25th birthday, what would you hope they would say about your influence in their life?"

Key Teaching Point 3: From Vision to Action - Your Fatherhood Plan (10 minutes)

Present a framework for turning vision into reality:

- Setting SMART goals in each of the five pillar areas
- Creating rhythms and routines that support your priorities
- Establishing accountability for your fatherhood journey
- Anticipating and planning for challenges and obstacles
- Regular evaluation and adjustment of your approach

Address common implementation challenges:

- Maintaining consistency amid life's demands
- Balancing multiple priorities
- Recovering from setbacks and failures
- Adapting as children grow and family circumstances change

Scripture focus: "The plans of the diligent lead to profit as surely as haste leads to poverty." (Proverbs 21:5)

Discussion prompt: "What specific rhythms or routines could you establish to ensure your fatherhood vision becomes reality?"

Small Group Application Exercise (10 minutes)

Distribute goal-setting worksheets.

Have each person:

- Write their personal fatherhood vision statement (2-3 sentences)
- Identify one SMART goal for each of the five pillars
- Share their vision and one key goal with their small group
- Group members offer supportive feedback and accountability suggestions.

Next Steps & Assignment Overview (5 minutes)

Explain that our final session next week will focus on celebration and long-term success. Encourage them to:

> ➢ Complete their full fatherhood plan with goals for each pillar
> ➢ Begin implementing at least one new rhythm or routine this week
> ➢ Reflect on how they will maintain momentum after our group concludes

Preview the final week's reading:

> ➢ Fathering Strong – God's Blueprint for Leading Your Family: Chapter 15
> ➢ Fathering Strong – 30-Day Devotional and Journal: Complete Week 3, Days 15-21

Close with a prayer for wisdom in implementing the fatherhood plans, courage to face challenges, and joy in the journey of intentional fatherhood.

Closing Prayer

Heavenly Father,

We stand before You today as men committed to becoming the fathers You've called us to be. As we develop our fatherhood plans and set goals for our families, we ask for Your divine wisdom to guide our steps.

Lord, grant us clarity of vision to see the fathers we can become through Your strength. Help us establish rhythms and routines that transform our good intentions into daily reality.

When we face obstacles and distractions that pull us from our purpose, give us courage to stay the course. In moments of failure or frustration, remind us that Your grace is sufficient and that growth comes through perseverance.

Father, infuse our journey with joy. Help us find delight in the daily moments of fatherhood— both the milestones and the mundane. Let our children see in us men who approach fatherhood not as a burden but as a blessed calling.

As we leave today, plant these plans deep in our hearts. Transform our learning into living, our goals into growth, and our vision into a vibrant legacy that honors You.

In Jesus' name, we pray, Amen.

Facilitation Notes and Tips

For the Welcome & Check-in: Create an atmosphere that celebrates progress while acknowledging that fatherhood is a continuous journey of growth. Affirm even small steps participants have taken.

For the Review of Previous Week's Assignment: Listen for how participants are integrating concepts from multiple sessions into their approach to building bonds with their children.

For the Core Teaching: When discussing fatherhood vision, emphasize that effective visions are both aspirational and realistic. Help participants create visions that inspire without overwhelming them.

Present goal-setting in ways that feel manageable rather than burdensome. Emphasize that the purpose of goals is to provide direction, not create pressure.

For the Small Group Exercise: If participants struggle with creating a vision statement, offer sentence starters like: "As a father, I want to be known for..." or "The most important things I want to give my children are..."

For the Next Steps: Remind participants that their fatherhood plan is a living document that will evolve as they and their children grow. The goal is progress, not perfection.

Potential Challenges and Solutions:

Challenge: Participant feels overwhelmed by trying to improve in all areas at once.
Solution: Encourage focus: "Start with the one area that would make the biggest difference for your family right now. Small, consistent changes in one area often create positive momentum in others."

Challenge: Participant expresses doubt about maintaining changes after the program ends.
Solution: Discuss sustainability strategies: "Consider what support structures you'll need to maintain these changes—whether that's an accountability partner, regular review times, or integrating new habits into existing routines."

Challenge: Participant struggles to articulate a clear vision.
Solution: Offer reflection questions: "Think about the fathers you admire. What qualities do they demonstrate? What impact do they have on their children? How might those observations inform your own fatherhood vision?"

Week 12: Building Your Legacy and Graduation

Session Preparation

Room Setup: Arrange seating in a circle or semi-circle to create a sense of community for this final session. Consider adding simple decorative elements to create a celebratory atmosphere.

Materials Needed:

➢ Participant Workbooks

➢ Certificates of Completion for each participant

➢ Whiteboard or flip chart

➢ Markers

➢ Legacy commitment cards

Optional: Refreshments for post-session celebration

Optional: Camera for group photo

Pre-Session Checklist:

➢ Pray for the session and participants

➢ Review teaching content and discussion questions

➢ Prepare personal examples that illustrate key points

➢ Set up room and any technology

➢ Arrange refreshments if provided

Session Outline (75 minutes)

Welcome & Celebration (10 minutes)

➢ Warmly welcome everyone to the final session with enthusiasm.

➢ Acknowledge the journey: "Twelve weeks ago, we gathered as men committed to becoming stronger fathers. Today, we celebrate the growth, insights, and commitments you've made along the way."

➢ Brief check-in: "In one sentence, share how this fatherhood journey has impacted you personally."

Review of Previous Week's Assignment (10 minutes)

➢ Ask: "What aspects of your fatherhood plan are you most excited to implement?"

➢ Invite 2-3 participants to share their completed fatherhood vision statements.

➢ Address any questions that arose from the reading or Week 3 of the devotional.

Core Teaching & Discussion (30 minutes)

Key Teaching Point 1: Understanding Legacy (10 minutes)

Define the concept of fatherhood legacy:

➢ The difference between leaving an inheritance and leaving a legacy

➢ How your influence extends beyond your lifetime

➢ The generational impact of faithful fatherhood

➢ Legacy as daily decisions, not just end-of-life considerations

Scripture focus: "A good person leaves an inheritance for their children's children, but a sinner's wealth is stored up for the righteous." (Proverbs 13:22)

Discussion prompt: "What aspects of your father's legacy do you want to carry forward, and what new legacy elements do you want to establish for your children?"

Key Teaching Point 2: The Four Components of a Lasting Legacy (10 minutes)

Present the framework for building a multi-dimensional legacy:

> ➤ Spiritual legacy: Faith values and relationship with God
> ➤ Character legacy: Integrity, work ethic, and personal virtues
> ➤ Relational legacy: How to love, resolve conflict, and build community
> ➤ Wisdom legacy: Life lessons, practical skills, and decision-making

Emphasize that legacy-building happens in both planned moments and everyday interactions.

Personal example: Share briefly about a legacy element you received from your father or are intentionally building with your children.

Discussion prompt: "Which of these four legacy components feels most natural for you to build, and which requires more intentional effort?"

Key Teaching Point 3: Sustaining Your Fatherhood Journey (10 minutes)

Provide strategies for long-term fatherhood success:

> ➤ The power of community and continued accountability
> ➤ Establishing regular times to review and adjust your fatherhood plan
> ➤ Celebrating milestones and progress with your family
> ➤ Recovering well from inevitable setbacks
> ➤ Growing alongside your children through different life stages

Address common long-term challenges:

> ➤ Maintaining momentum after initial enthusiasm
> ➤ Adapting approaches as children grow older
> ➤ Balancing consistency with flexibility
> ➤ Finding support during difficult seasons

Scripture focus: "Let us not become weary in doing good, for at the proper time we will reap a harvest if we do not give up." (Galatians 6:9)

Discussion prompt: "What specific support structures will help you maintain your fatherhood commitments in the months and years ahead?"

Legacy Commitment Ceremony (15 minutes)

Distribute legacy commitment cards.

Explain: "This commitment represents your intention to continue the fatherhood journey we've begun together."

Ask each man to write on his card:

> ➤ One sentence describing the father he commits to becoming
> ➤ Three specific actions he will take in the next 30 days
> ➤ A scripture that will guide his fatherhood journey
> ➤ Invite participants to form a circle and share their commitments one by one.
> ➤ After all have shared, lead a prayer of blessing over the fathers and their families.

Introduction to the 30-Day Devotional Journey (5 minutes)

Congratulations! You have now completed the Fathering Strong workshop and the Fatherhood Awakening exercises. This marks not an ending but a beginning of your intentional fatherhood journey.

You are now ready to embark on a 30-day journey through the devotional and journal. This is where you'll take everything you've learned and put it into action through your SMART goals to become the best dad you can be. Each day provides an opportunity to reinforce the principles we've discussed and implement them in practical ways with your children.

To support you during this crucial implementation phase, we've created opportunities to connect with each other over the next 30 days using the Fathering Strong app. There, you can share victories, ask questions, and encourage one another as you apply these principles in your daily life.

Graduation and Next Steps (5 minutes)

Present certificates of completion to each participant, sharing a brief personal observation about their growth or contribution to the group.

Discuss potential next steps:

> ➤ Monthly follow-up gatherings
> ➤ Forming ongoing accountability partnerships within the Fathering Strong app community
> ➤ Opportunities to mentor new fathers
> ➤ Resources for continued growth
> ➤ Take a group photo to commemorate the journey.
> ➤ Close with a final prayer of commissioning for the fathers.

Closing Prayer

Heavenly Father,

Today, we stand before You as men forever changed by the journey we've shared. We thank You for bringing us together, for the bonds we've formed, and for the transformation You've begun in our hearts as fathers.

Lord, as these men return to their homes and families, commission them with Your authority and purpose. May they walk with a new confidence, not in their own strength, but in Your unfailing guidance and grace.

Lord, anoint their words with power to speak life and identity into their children. Strengthen their hands to lead with both gentleness and conviction. Guard their hearts against discouragement and doubt.

We pray You would multiply the seeds planted during this workshop. May the principles learned here take deep root and bear fruit for generations to come. When challenges arise—and they will—remind these fathers of Your presence and the community that stands with them.

Lord, help these men to be intentional architects of legacy, emotional shepherds to their children's hearts, and wise stewards of all You've entrusted to them. May they lead their families with vision, vulnerability, and unwavering commitment.

As they leave this place, send them forth as ambassadors of authentic fatherhood in a world desperate for their influence. May their example inspire other men to embrace their calling as fathers.

We commission these men not to perfection but to faithful presence—showing up day after day, reflecting Your Father's heart to a watching world.

In the mighty name of Jesus, the perfect revelation of the Father's heart, we pray, Amen.

Conclusion: The Impact of Your Leadership

As we conclude this facilitator's guide, we want to express our deepest gratitude for your commitment to leading this Fathering Strong workshop. The time, energy, and heart you've invested in these fathers will create ripples that extend far beyond what you may ever see.

By guiding these men through their fatherhood journey, you've helped strengthen not just individual families but entire communities. When fathers lead with purpose, wisdom, and love, they create secure environments where children can thrive. These children grow up with a stronger sense of identity, purpose, and belonging—qualities our communities desperately need.

Your willingness to facilitate vulnerable conversations, share wisdom, and create a space for authentic growth has made a profound difference. Some of the fathers in your group may have never experienced positive male mentorship before. Through your example, they've gained not just information but transformation.

The legacy being built through your leadership will impact generations. Children who might never have known the security of engaged fatherhood will now experience it. And those children will likely become parents who pass on these same values to their children.

Thank you for making your local families stronger, your community healthier, and for contributing to a movement of intentional fatherhood that has the power to change our culture. The investment you've made in these fathers is immeasurable, and its returns will continue to multiply for years to come.

Your service matters. Your leadership matters. And the fathers you've guided are better men, better husbands, and better fathers because of your influence. Thank you!

Notes

For more resources, go to:

www.fatheringstrongbook.com

Purchase the book that accompanies this workshop

Fathering Strong – God's Blueprint for Leading Your Family

Purchase online at all major book outlets.

12-week Workshop for Churches

Interested in starting a fatherhood class? Participant Workbooks and Facilitator Guides are available with the book and other resources. Certificates are available for participants. Contact information@fatheringstrongbook.com for bundle discounts.

Join a fatherhood community where you can connect with other fathers, get support and encouragement throughout your fatherhood journey, and become empowered to be the best dad you can be. Join this free community today!

Join at www.fatheringstrong.com